Piecing Art Together

Dona Herweck Rice

✹ Smithsonian

Contributing Author

Jennifer Lawson

Consultants

Emily Key
Education Programs Manager
Smithsonian Latino Center

Sharon Banks
3rd Grade Teacher
Duncan Public Schools

Publishing Credits

Rachelle Cracchiolo, M.S.Ed., *Publisher*
Conni Medina, M.A.Ed., *Managing Editor*
Diana Kenney, M.A.Ed., NBCT, *Content Director*
Véronique Bos, *Creative Director*
Robin Erickson, *Art Director*
Michelle Jovin, M.A., *Associate Editor*
Mindy Duits, *Senior Graphic Designer*
Smithsonian Science Education Center

Image Credits: front cover, p.1, p.19 Zuma Press/Alamy; pp.2–3 Gary Cameron/
Reuters/Newscom; p.7 (bottom) Courtesy Tonya Corkey; p.9 dpa picture alliance
archive/Alamy; p.11 (top) Courtesy Metropolitan Transportation Authority
of the State of New York; p.12 Wonderlane; p.13 Riccardo Sala/agefotostock/
Newscom; p.18 © WashedAshore.org; p.20 (left) Getty Images; p.20 (right)
Underawesternsky/Shutterstock; p.21 James Michael Dorsey/Shutterstock; p.21
(insert) BB Prince/Shutterstock; p.22 (bottom) Bob Chamberlin/Los Angeles Times
via Getty Images; p.23 Levi Clancy; p.24 Robyn Beck/AFP/Getty Images; p.25
(top) Marie Appert/iStock; p.25 (bottom) Lucas Jackson/Reuters/Newscom; p.26
Alistair Heap/Alamy; p.27 (top) Reuters/Newscom; p.27 (middle) Imaginechina/
Newscom; p.27 (bottom left) Li Changxiang Xinhua News Agency/Newscom; all
other images from iStock and/or Shutterstock.

Library of Congress Cataloging-in-Publication Data

Names: Rice, Dona, author.
Title: Piecing art together / Dona Herweck Rice.
Description: Huntington Beach, CA : Teacher Created Materials, Inc., 2019. |
 Includes index. | Audience: K to Grade 3. |
Identifiers: LCCN 2018030740 (print) | LCCN 2018036814 (ebook) | ISBN
 9781493869046 (E-book) | ISBN 9781493866649 (pbk.)
Subjects: LCSH: Artists' materials--Juvenile literature. | Art--Juvenile
 literature.
Classification: LCC N8530 (ebook) | LCC N8530 .R53 2019 (print) | DDC
 702.8--dc23
LC record available at https://lccn.loc.gov/2018030740

◉ Smithsonian

Teacher Created Materials

5301 Oceanus Drive
Huntington Beach, CA 92649-1030
www.tcmpub.com
ISBN 978-1-4938-6664-9
©2019 Teacher Created Materials, Inc.

Table of Contents

3

Look Around

Hundreds of feathers cover a blue jay. Thousands of leaves cover a tree. Millions of grains of sand cover a beach.

Look around. The world is filled with small things that combine to make big and beautiful things. Art can be like that too. In fact, some artists only work with little **bits** to create big works of art!

blue jay

maple tree

grains of sand

From Found to Fab

Most artists make art in common **mediums**. They use things such as paint and clay. Other artists use different mediums. They might make art from things they find. They look for beauty in found objects. For example, some art is made from dryer **lint**! Bits and pieces of nature are also used.

An artist makes jars out of clay.

An artist uses paint on a canvas.

Lint

Lint comes off in clothes dryers. The color of lint depends on the color of fabrics being dried. Each color of lint can be used as it is or mixed to create works of art.

This art piece by Tonya Corkey is made with dryer lint.

Artists can find art everywhere they look. They might find trash or broken pieces of glass and turn them into art. They might shape the pieces into things you know. Or, they might form patterns.

What artists make can be silly or serious. Art can serve a purpose or just be fun to look at. But no matter what, it is still art!

These pieces of trash and recycled materials can be turned into works of art.

This work of art by HA Schult is called *Trash People*.

Marvelous Mosaics

Mosaics are works of art made from many small tiles, rocks, glass pieces, shells, or beads. Artists use these bits and pieces to form pictures or patterns.

Mosaics may be used to make things, such as floors or walls. They may also be used just as art. They can be any size, shape, or color.

An artist adds tiles to a mosaic.

This glass mosaic is on a wall in one of Germany's subway stations.

Making Mosaics

Artists first measure how big a mosaic can be based on its location. That helps them know how many pieces they need. Then, they compare the shapes of pieces they have. That helps them fit shapes together. Lastly, artists add **grout** between pieces to keep them in place.

Made to Last

People have made mosaics since **ancient** times. Some very old ones can be found in museums. Some still exist in old buildings. Many of them are **intact**. The pieces have stayed in place all these years.

Mosaics today are often made as they were long ago. Techniques have not changed much. Hopefully today's mosaics will last just as long!

Some **monks** make sand mosaics, called mandalas.

Museum guests learn about the Ishtar Gate, a mosaic built around 575 BC.

Patience

Artists who make mosaics must be patient. Each piece has to be the right size and shape. It also must be placed in just the right way. One piece out of place can affect the whole design. It is best for artists to make a good plan before setting any piece in place. They take the time to get it right.

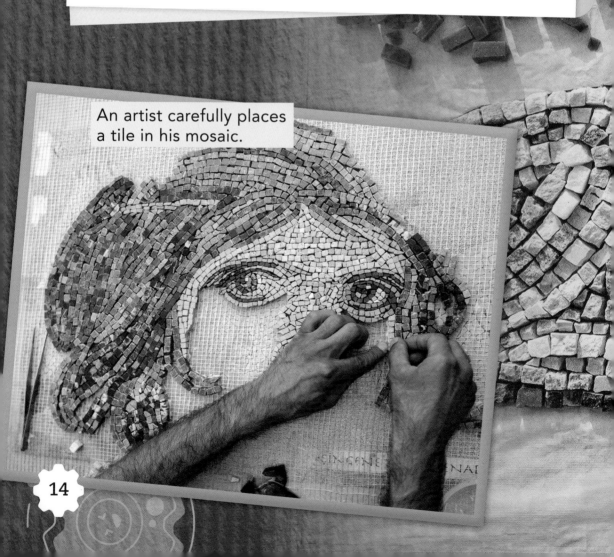

An artist carefully places a tile in his mosaic.

An artist places the last piece of rock in her lion mosaic.

15

Ocean Trash to Treasure

There is a lot of trash floating in oceans around the world. Most of that trash is plastic. People are concerned about what this trash does to ocean life. It can be deadly. Some artists want to bring attention to the problem. So, what do they do? They make art!

This elephant statue is made of plastic water bottles.

North Pacific

**Subtropical
Convergence Zone**

Kuroshio

Western Garbage Patch

California

**Eastern Garbage Patch or
N. Pacific Subtropical High**

North Equatorial

Ocean currents move plastic into
clumps called garbage patches.

A sea turtle eats
a plastic bag.

The Washed Ashore Project makes art from plastic found in oceans. One of its sculptures is a parrot fish. Its name is Priscilla. The artist matched all the colors and shapes to make a huge fish. The fish is bright and fun. But it also has a story to tell. It does not say a word. But it lets people know it is not okay to dump trash in the oceans!

A Washed Ashore artist starts building a sculpture.

Priscilla the Parrot Fish

Getting Rid of Plastic

Plastic takes hundreds of years
to **decompose**. Scientists are
working to make a new kind of
plastic. They hope to find a way to
make it break down faster.

19

Piece by Piece

Some artists make huge works of art by doing it one piece at a time. Simon Rodia did that. He built giant metal towers in his yard. They are covered with bits of glass, tile, and other things. Rodia found the objects near his home. He used cement to make the pieces stick.

Rodia made 17 towers. It took him 33 years! The towers are in California. They are now known as the Watts Towers.

This is the entrance to the Watts Towers.

Simon Rodia builds one of his Watts Towers.

Watts Towers

close-up of one of the Watts Towers

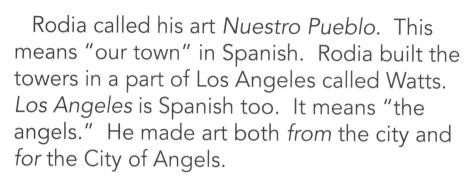

Rodia called his art *Nuestro Pueblo*. This means "our town" in Spanish. Rodia built the towers in a part of Los Angeles called Watts. *Los Angeles* is Spanish too. It means "the angels." He made art both *from* the city and *for* the City of Angels.

The Watts Towers still stand. But over time, the sun has harmed them. People are working to keep the towers safe. The towers are part of the city's story.

Workers try to fix damage on one of the Watts Towers.

Saving the Towers

Heat from the sun causes the Watts Towers to move a little each day. This causes the cement on the towers to crack. Engineers are trying to find a substance to fill the cracks. It must bend but still hold the towers together.

Near Los Angeles, there are more art pieces that are built piece by piece. And these works of art are moving! There is a parade that takes place each New Year's Day. The Tournament of Roses Parade® is filled with **floats**. The floats are covered with flowers and other plant life. Hundreds of helpers make these works of art.

Workers cover the floats with millions of flowers, leaves, and seeds. They put each piece on one at a time. But the plants do not last long. New floats are made each year.

The Rose Parade has many colorful floats every year.

This Rose Parade float was built by the Natural History Museum of Los Angeles County.

HAPPY NEW YEAR

A volunteer puts a rose onto a float.

Art Is Where You Find It

Anything can be used to make art! Many people have made art from small plastic bricks, but could they have used toothpicks? What about cereal or toast? These have all been used to craft works of art!

Art can be anything, and it can be found anywhere. Look around. Where do you find a work of art?

Artist Nathan Wyburn adds toast to his art of British royal Kate Middleton.

Making art from found objects may have started in France. That practice was called *objet trouvé*, or "found object."

This statue of comic book hero The Flash® was made of plastic bricks in France in 2018.

This statue of video game character Yoshi® was made of soup cans in New York in 2015.

Artist Liu Xuedong stands with his horse made of toothpicks.

Tomato & Red Pepper Soup

STEAM CHALLENGE

Define the Problem

Your town is having a Trash-to-Treasure day. People have asked you to design a sculpture.

 Constraints: You must use at least 10 items to make your sculpture. You must use items that most people would put in the trash. You may use tape or glue to hold the parts together.

 Criteria: Your sculpture must be able to stand on its own for at least 15 seconds.

Research and Brainstorm

Why should you have patience when creating art? What types of items might be considered trash? How can you make your sculpture stand?

Design and Build

Collect at least 10 pieces of trash for your artwork. What purpose will each part serve? What materials will work best? Create your sculpture.

Test and Improve

Show your design to your friends. Did your sculpture use 10 items of trash? Did it stand for 15 seconds? How can you improve it? Improve your design and try again.

Reflect and Share

Why should people make art with items from the trash? How else can people turn trash into something new?

Glossary

ancient—refers to something from a time long ago

bits—small pieces of things

decompose—to slowly break down by natural processes

floats—vehicles with platforms that carry displays in parades

grout—a material used for filling cracks or spaces between small pieces

intact—not broken

lint—tiny pieces of cloth or other soft materials that can be found in clothes dryers

mediums—methods or materials used by artists

monks—male members of some religious groups who live separate from society, usually without money

Index

Career Advice
from Smithsonian

Do you want to be an artist?
Here are some tips to get you started.

"Ask questions and talk to people. Try new things, and you can be a great artist!" —*Emily Key, Education Programs Manager*

"To be a great artist, you need to know about a lot of subjects, such as history and science. Study hard and start creating!" —*Diane Kidd, Illustrator and Museum Educator*